Facts About the Boa Constrictor

By Lisa Strattin

© 2016 Lisa Strattin

Revised 2022 © Lisa Strattin

FREE BOOK

FREE FOR ALL SUBSCRIBERS

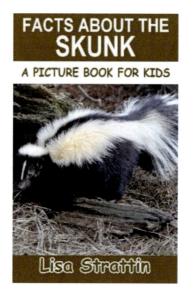

LisaStrattin.com/Subscribe-Here

BOX SET

- **FACTS ABOUT THE POISON DART FROGS**
- **FACTS ABOUT THE THREE TOED SLOTH**
  - **FACTS ABOUT THE RED PANDA**
  - **FACTS ABOUT THE SEAHORSE**
  - **FACTS ABOUT THE PLATYPUS**
  - **FACTS ABOUT THE REINDEER**
  - **FACTS ABOUT THE PANTHER**
- **FACTS ABOUT THE SIBERIAN HUSKY**

LisaStrattin.com/BookBundle

Facts for Kids Picture Books by Lisa Strattin

Little Blue Penguin, Vol 92

Chipmunk, Vol 5

Frilled Lizard, Vol 39

Blue and Gold Macaw, Vol 13

Poison Dart Frogs, Vol 50

Blue Tarantula, Vol 115

African Elephants, Vol 8

Amur Leopard, Vol 89

Sabre Tooth Tiger, Vol 167

Baboon, Vol 174

Sign Up for New Release Emails Here

LisaStrattin.com/subscribe-here

All rights reserved. No part of this book may be reproduced by any means whatsoever without the written permission from the author, except brief portions quoted for purpose of review.

All information in this book has been carefully researched and checked for factual accuracy. However, the author and publisher makes no warranty, express or implied, that the information contained herein is appropriate for every individual, situation or purpose and assume no responsibility for errors or omissions. The reader assumes the risk and full responsibility for all actions, and the author will not be held responsible for any loss or damage, whether consequential, incidental, special or otherwise, that may result from the information presented in this book.

All images are free for use or purchased from stock photo sites or royalty free for commercial use.

Some coloring pages might be of the general species due to lack of available images.

I have relied on my own observations as well as many different sources for this book and I have done my best to check facts and give credit where it is due. In the event that any material is used without proper permission, please contact me so that the oversight can be corrected.

COVER IMAGE

https://www.flickr.com/photos/92252798@N07/15601494756/

ADDTIIONAL IMAGES

https://www.flickr.com/photos/zapmole/40440485121/

https://www.flickr.com/photos/189441894@N06/50145316113/

https://www.flickr.com/photos/110608682@N04/31857359002/

https://www.flickr.com/photos/dsevictoria/4765758515/

https://www.flickr.com/photos/dusantos_bh/1271272034/

https://www.flickr.com/photos/dusantos_bh/1271355826/

https://www.flickr.com/photos/wildlife_encounters/13868586163/

https://www.flickr.com/photos/shankaronline/16257931429/

https://www.flickr.com/photos/vsmithuk/7525980432/

https://www.flickr.com/photos/allenthepostman/3264149478/

Contents

INTRODUCTION 9

CHARACTERISTICS 11

APPEARANCE 13

LIFE STAGES 15

LIFE SPAN 17

SIZE 19

HABITAT 21

DIET 23

FRIENDS AND ENEMIES 25

SUITABILITY AS PETS 27

INTRODUCTION

The Boa Constrictor belongs to the family of snakes which has no venom; they capture their prey and kill it by squeezing off the blood circulation and constricting it. They are reptiles and are distinct to all reptiles. They are the close relatives of Anaconda but not long like the Anaconda.

CHARACTERISTICS

The Boa Constrictor is usually found in tropical Central and South America, and it is a great swimmer. Usually, they are found on dry land because they prefer to live there. They make their homes in abandoned mammal burrows and inside of hollow logs.

They have small teeth, lined up in their jaws, which are used to grab the food. They grab their prey and wrap their muscular body around it, blocking the respiratory tract and blood flow, squeezing it until it suffocates. They also have ability to re-grow their teeth. This is a gift of nature for the Boa Constrictors so that when they grow old, their teeth fall out, but they regrow new ones!

APPEARANCE

The appearance of Boa Constrictors depends on their habitat. They are green, tan, yellow, or red, according to where they are living. The average size of a Boa Constrictor is just less than 10 feet long. But the longest Boa Constrictor recorded is 13 feet. According to research, females are larger than males.

The appearance of a Boa Constrictor is significantly different from Anacondas. They have markings on their body which spread all over the whole body. Those markings can vary in color from dark brown to green.

LIFE STAGES

This kind of snake is a seasonal breeder, and their female excretes a scent to attract the males. Fertilization occurs internally and after this, the female gives birth. Females develop the embryo inside the body, and the babies are born independent.

The color of Boa Constrictors may change when it grows older and their skin sheds, so young snakes have brighter colors than older ones.

LIFE SPAN

The life span of Boa Constrictor can be 20 to 30 years long whether they are in the wild or kept as a pet.

SIZE

The average size of Boa Constrictors is shorter than their relative, the Anaconda. The average size of an Anaconda is about 20 feet while the average Boa Constrictors are just less than 10 feet long.

Even though it is shorter than the Anaconda, it is a long snake!

HABITAT

Boa Constrictors are found in several different environments and their habitats vary widely. They live in rainforests as well as in arid semi-desert country. The tropical, rainforest regions are preferred because they enjoy the humidity and temperature, but they are also found on riversides and in dry areas.

DIET

The Boa Constrictor is a reptile and is a predator because its diet includes small to medium sized mammals and birds. They like to eat rodents, lizards, and even larger mammals like ocelots.

When the snake is young, its diet consists of small mice, bats, lizards, and amphibians. As it gets older, the diet changes and it begins to eat large mammals and birds. They are natural hunters and do most of their hunting at night. It waits for its catch to die while constricting it, and then consumes it.

The meals of Boa Constrictors digest in 4 to 6 days. Because of this, the Boa Constrictor can go for many days without eating anything at all.

FRIENDS AND ENEMIES

Many larger animals are the enemies of Boa Constrictor. It can also be attacked by other snakes, but it doesn't happen that often.

Usually, the Boa Constrictor is the enemy of other mammals and birds. But large predatory birds like to eat Boa Constrictors.

People can be an enemy of Boa Constrictors – but they can also be their friend because lots of people keep the Boa Constrictor as a pet.

SUITABILITY AS PETS

There are many people who keep a Boa Constrictor as a pet. As a matter of fact, they are a very popular snake to keep as a pet for people who enjoy having snakes. They do need special care and training because Boa Constrictors will try to escape their caged surroundings.

If you choose to keep a Boa Constrictor as a pet, you will enjoy the snake's company, but you must also always be aware of the dangers and take appropriate precautions for your safety and the safety of your pet.

COLOR ME

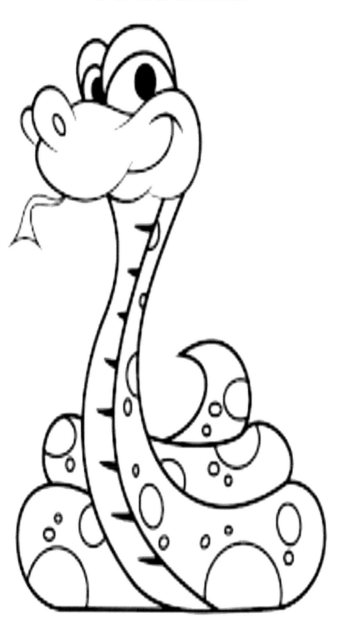

COLOR ME

COLOR ME

COLOR ME

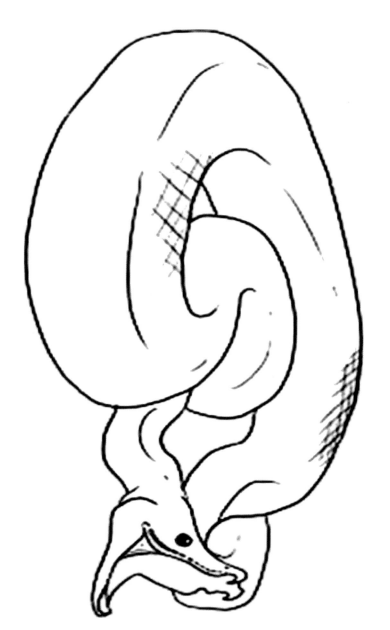

COLOR ME

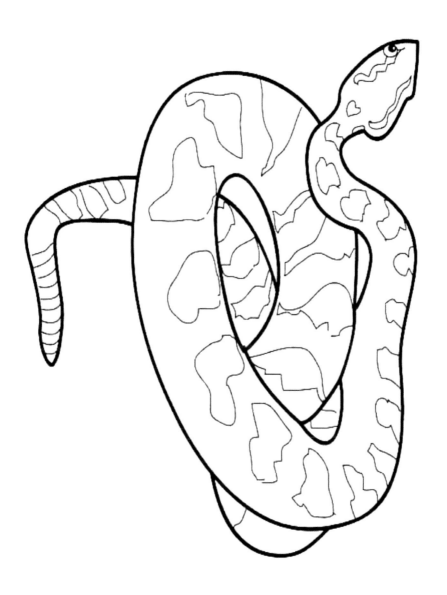

COLOR ME

COLOR ME

COLOR ME

COLOR ME

COLOR ME

Please leave me a review here:

LisaStrattin.com/Review-Vol-24

For more Kindle Downloads Visit Lisa Strattin Author Page on Amazon Author Central

amazon.com/author/lisastrattin

To see upcoming titles, visit my website at LisaStrattin.com– most books available on Kindle!

LisaStrattin.com

FREE BOOK

FOR ALL SUBSCRIBERS – SIGN UP NOW

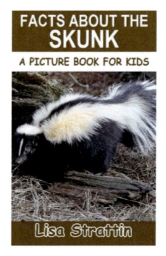

LisaStrattin.com/Subscribe-Here

LisaStrattin.com/Facebook

LisaStrattin.com/Youtube

Made in the USA
Middletown, DE
01 April 2023